LITTLE JAMIE BOOK

What It's Like to Be...

*Qué se siente al ser...*

WITHDRAWN

# CAMERON DÍAZ

BY/POR
**TAMMY GAGNE**

TRANSLATED BY/
TRADUCIDO POR
**EIDA DE LA VEGA**

**Mitchell Lane**
PUBLISHERS

P.O. Box 196
Hockessin, Delaware 19707
Visit us on the web: www.mitchelllane.com
Comments? Email us:
mitchelllane@mitchelllane.com

## Mitchell Lane
### PUBLISHERS

Printing          1          2          3          4          5          6          7          8          9

## A LITTLE JAMIE BOOK

What It's Like to Be . . .                    Qué se siente al ser . . .

| | |
|---|---|
| América Ferrera | América Ferrera |
| Cameron Díaz | Cameron Díaz |
| George López | George López |
| Jennifer López | Jennifer López |
| The Jonas Brothers | Los Hermanos Jonas |
| Kaká | Kaká |
| Mariano Rivera | Mariano Rivera |
| Mark Sánchez | Mark Sánchez |
| Marta Vieira | Marta Vieira |
| Miley Cyrus | Miley Cyrus |
| Óscar De La Hoya | Óscar De La Hoya |
| Pelé | Pelé |
| President Barack Obama | El presidente Barack Obama |
| Ryan Howard | Ryan Howard |
| Selena Gómez | Selena Gómez |
| Shakira | Shakira |
| Sonia Sotomayor | Sonia Sotomayor |
| Vladimir Guerrero | Vladimir Guerrero |

Library of Congress Cataloging-in-Publication Data
Gagne, Tammy.
 What it's like to be Cameron Díaz  / by Tammy Gagne ; translated by Eida de la Vega = ¿Qué se siente al ser Cameron Díaz? / por Tammy Gagne ; traducido por Eida de la Vega.
    p. cm. — (A little Jamie book = Un libro "little Jamie")
 Includes bibliographical references and index.
 ISBN 978-1-61228-323-4 (library bound)
1.  Díaz, Cameron—Juvenile literature. 2.  Motion picture actors and actresses—United States—Biography—Juvenile literature. I. Vega, Eida de la. II. Title. III. Title: ¿Qué se siente al ser Cameron Díaz?. IV. Title: What it's like to be Cameron Díaz.
 PN2287.D4633G34 2012
 791.4302'8'092—dc23
 [B]
                                                                                    2012028100

eBook ISBN: 9781612283937

What It's Like to Be... /
Qué se siente al ser...

# CAMERON
# DÍAZ

Shrek

When you hear Cameron Diaz speak, she might sound familiar. Cameron is the voice of Princess Fiona from the *Shrek* movies.

Fiona

Cuando escuchas la voz de Cameron Díaz, te puede sonar familiar. Cameron es la voz de la princesa Fiona en las películas de Shrek.

5

You also may have seen Cameron on the Nickelodeon Kids' Choice Awards. In recent years, she has won both the Burp Award and the Wannabe Award at this fun ceremony. She has also hosted the show with her *Shrek* co-star Mike Myers.

Wannabe Award/ *Premio Wannabe*

*También puedes haber visto a Cameron en los Premios Kids' Choice de Nickelodeon. En años recientes, ha ganado el Premio Burp (Eructo) y el Premio Wannabe (Quiero ser) en esta divertida ceremonia. También ha sido la presentadora de este espectáculo con su co-protagonista de Shrek, Mike Myers.*

Cameron and Mike Meyers team up again to host the 17th Annual Kids' Choice Awards.

*Cameron y Mike Myers se unen otra vez para presentar los XVII Premios Anuales Kids' Choice.*

Mike Myers

Cameron Michelle Díaz was born on August 30, 1972, in San Diego, California. Her parents, Emilio and Billie, already had one daughter when Cameron joined the family. Her sister, Chimene, is two years older than she is.

Cameron Michelle Díaz nació el 30 de agosto de 1972 en San Diego, California. Sus padres, Emilio y Billie, ya tenían una hija cuando Cameron entró a la familia. Su hermana, Chimene, es dos años mayor que ella.

Sister/
*Hermana*
Chimene

9

Cameron makes an appearance on *El Hormiguero*, a television show in Madrid, Spain.

*Cameron hace una aparición en El Hormiguero, un programa de televisión en Madrid, España.*

Cameron's mother is from a German, British, and Native American family. Her father was Cuban-American. "Because I'm blonde and blue-eyed, people can't believe that I am a Latina," she tells *Scholastic Action*. Cameron's heritage is important to her. "Being Latin is part of who I am."

*La madre de Cameron tiene ascendencia alemana, inglesa y nativoamericana. Su padre era cubanoamericano. "Como soy rubia y de ojos azules, la gente no cree que soy latina", le dice a la revista Scholastic Action. Para Cameron, sus raíces son muy importantes. "Ser latina forma parte de quien soy".*

Cameron is very close with her family. "I talk to my mom constantly – sometimes several times a day," she shares with *Scholastic Action*. Sadly, her father passed away unexpectedly in 2008. Cameron says that his humor will always live in her heart. "I can shut my eyes and hear my father's laugh," she tells *Biography*.

Cameron está muy apegada a su familia. "Le hablo a mi mamá constantemente, en ocasiones, varias veces al día", comparte con Scholastic Action. Por desgracia, su padre murió repentinamente en el 2008. Cameron dice que el humor de su padre siempre vivirá en su corazón. "Cierro los ojos y puedo escuchar la risa de mi padre", le dice a Biography.

Cameron's family/ *La familia de Cameron*

Cameron has starred in more than 30 movies. Many have been romantic comedies, like *My Best Friend's Wedding* and *Knight and Day*. She has a great talent for humor, perhaps because she grew up with so much laughter. "That's the way it was in my house," she tells *Scholastic Action*. "To survive, you just had to laugh."

*Cameron ha protagonizado más de 30 películas. Muchas han sido comedias románticas como* La boda de mi mejor amigo *y* Encuentro explosivo. *Ella tiene mucho talento para el humor, quizás porque creció con muchas risas a su alrededor. "Así era en mi casa", le dice a Scholastic Action. "Para sobrevivir, sólo tenías que reírte".*

Actor /
*Actor*
Tom
Cruise

Actor/
*Actor*
Jim
Carrey

Cameron didn't always want to be an actress. She started out as a model when she was 16 years old. She did ad campaigns for companies like Calvin Klein and Coca-Cola. It was her modeling agent who suggested she try out for a role in *The Mask.* This comedy with Jim Carrey became her first movie.

*Cameron no siempre quiso ser actriz. Empezó como modelo a los 16 años. Hizo campañas promocionales para compañías como Calvin Klein y Coca-Cola. Fue su agente de modelaje quien le sugirió que se presentara para un papel en La máscara. Esta comedia con Jim Carrey fue su primera película.*

Cameron Díaz as Lotte Schwartz in *Being John Malkovich* / *Cameron Díaz como Lotte Schwartz en ¿Quieres ser John Malkovich?*

Since *The Mask,* Cameron has won many different film roles. When Cameron played Lotte Schwartz in *Being John Malkovich,* she looked so different that many people didn't even recognize her. In *My Sister's Keeper,* she played the mother of a girl with cancer.

*A partir de* La máscara, *Cameron ha obtenido muchos papeles diferentes en películas. Cuando Cameron hizo de Lotte Schwartz en* ¿Quieres ser John Malkovich? *lucía tan diferente que mucha gente ni siquiera la reconoció. En* La decisión más difícil *hacía de la madre de una niña con cáncer.*

Actress/
*Actriz*
Sofia
Vassilieva

Actress/
*Actriz*
Abigail
Breslin

Actress and singer/
*Actriz y cantante*
Jennifer López

Cameron and Jennifer López present an Academy Award to J. Roy Helland for Best Makeup.

Cameron y Jennifer López presentan un Premio de la Academia por Mejor Maquillaje a J. Roy Helland.

As a celebrity, Cameron goes to a lot of special events like award ceremonies and movie premieres. She joined Jennifer López at the 2012 Academy Awards to present the awards for Best Costume Design and Best Makeup.

*Como es una persona famosa, Cameron va a muchos eventos especiales como ceremonias de premiación y estrenos de películas. Apareció junto a Jennifer López en los Premios de la Academia 2012 para presentar los premios a Mejor Diseño de Vestuario y Mejor Maquillaje.*

When she isn't working, Cameron enjoys being a regular person. Jeans are her favorite clothes to wear. "Don't even ask me how many pairs I have," she jokes with *Harper's Bazaar*. Unlike many celebrities, she doesn't like to take advantage of being a star. She doesn't believe in cutting lines, taking things that are offered to her for free, or shutting down stores so she can shop in private.

*Cuando no está trabajando, Cameron disfruta ser una persona común y corriente. Su ropa preferida son los vaqueros. "Ni me pregunten cuántos pares tengo", bromea con la revista Harper's Bazaar. A diferencia de otras celebridades, a ella no le gusta aprovecharse de su fama. No cree en saltarse las filas, poniéndose delante de los demás, aceptar cosas gratis o hacer cerrar tiendas para poder comprar con privacidad.*

Actor/
*Actor*
Guy
Pearce

Even though she was once a model, Cameron doesn't focus on trying to be thin. Her co-workers describe her as a meat-and-potatoes girl. She accepts this label with her trademark humor. "I give every French fry a fair chance," she tells *Biography*.

*Aunque fue modelo, Cameron no se enfoca en tratar de estar delgada. Sus compañeros de trabajo la describen como una chica de carne con papas. Ella acepta esta etiqueta con su típico humor. "Yo le doy una oportunidad a cada papa frita", cuenta a Biography.*

Cameron says that she inherited her love of sports from her father. "He was a huge football fan," she tells *Access Hollywood*. "Dad didn't have a son, so my sister and I sort of absorbed his love of sports." One of her favorites is surfing. She got to show off her surfing skills in the movie *Charlie's Angels*.

Cameron dice que heredó su amor a los deportes de su padre. "Era tremendo aficionado al fútbol americano", le cuenta a Access Hollywood. "Papá no tuvo hijos, así que mi hermana y yo vinimos a absorber su amor a los deportes". Uno de sus favoritos en el surf. Pudo mostrar sus destrezas para surfear en Los ángeles de Charlie.

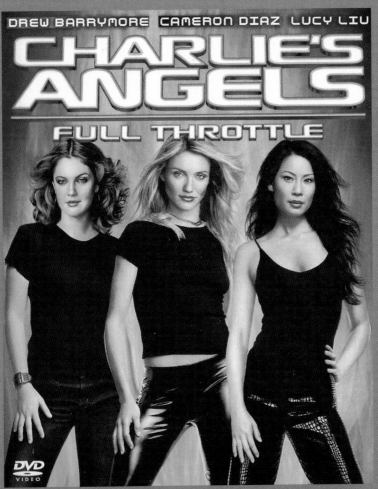

In her spare time, Cameron enjoys participating in different charity events. Many of them involve sports. She has competed in the Toyota Pro Celebrity Race to support children's hospitals in the United States. She also took part in *NSYNC's Challenge for the Children basketball game.

*En su tiempo libre, a Cameron le gusta participar en diferentes eventos caritativos. Muchos de ellos están relacionados con deportes. Compitió en la Carrera de Celebridades Toyota Pro para apoyar los hospitales para niños en Estados Unidos. También participó en el juego de baloncesto *NSYNC's Challenge for the Children.*

Musician/
*Músico*
Vince Neil

Actress/
*Actriz*
Shannon
Elizabeth

Cameron
Díaz

29

So what's next for this famous movie star with simple tastes? Even she doesn't know for sure, but two things are certain: First, it is sure to be something fun. Second, whatever it is, it will be on her terms. "I try to represent who I am . . ." she tells *InStyle*, "and to never be something I'm not."

¿Y qué vendrá ahora para esta famosa estrella de cine de gustos sencillos? Aunque ella misma no lo sepa, dos cosas son ciertas. Primero, seguro que algo divertido. Segundo, lo que sea, será como ella quiera. "Trato de representar quien soy", le dice a InStyle, "y nunca ser algo que no soy".

# FURTHER READING/LECTURAS RECOMENDADAS

Horn, Geoffrey M. *Cameron Diaz*. New York: Gareth Stevens Publishing, 2005.

International Movie Database (IMBd): Cameron Diaz. http://www.imdb.com/name/nm0000139/

People, http://www.people.com/people/cameron_diaz/0,,,00.html

Shrek.com, http://www.shrek.com/

## WORKS CONSULTED/
## OBRAS CONSULTADAS

Brown, Laura. "Cameron Diaz: Woman on Top." *Harper's Bazaar*, August 2010.

Cameron Diaz: Biography. http://www.biography.com/people/cameron-diaz-9273866

"Cameron Diaz Isn't Ready for Kids . . . Yet." *Access Hollywood*, May 28, 2009. http://today.msnbc.msn.com/id/30986071/ns/today-entertainment/t/cameron-diaz-isnt-ready-kids-yet/

"Cameron Diaz's Father Dies of Pneumonia." *TMZ*, April 15, 2008. http://www.tmz.com/2008/04/15/cameron-diazs-father-dies-from-pneumonia/

Davis, Ivor. "Giddy, Gorgeous, and Just One of the Guys: Cameron Diaz." *Biography*, April 2000.

Jones, Zach. "Cameron Diaz." *Scholastic Action*, September 15, 2008.

"Star Style Cameron Diaz." *InStyle UK*. http://www.instyle.co.uk/instyle/star-style-cameron-diaz/cameron-diaz3-star-style

# INDEX/ÍNDICE

**ABOUT THE AUTHOR:** Tammy Gagne has written numerous children's books about athletes, including *What It's Like to Be Pelé* and *What It's Like to Be Óscar De La Hoya* for Mitchell Lane Publishers. She resides in northern New England with her husband and son.
**ACERCA DE LA AUTORA:** Tammy Gagne ha escrito numerosos libros para niños, incluyendo *¿Qué se siente al ser Pelé?* y *¿Qué se siente al ser Óscar De La Hoya?* para Mitchell Lane Publishers. Vive en el norte de Nueva Inglaterra con su esposo y su hijo.

**ABOUT THE TRANSLATOR:** Eida de la Vega was born in Havana, Cuba, and now lives in New Jersey with her mother, her husband, and her two children. Eida has worked at Lectorum/Scholastic, and as editor of the magazine *Selecciones del Reader's Digest.*
**ACERCA DE LA TRADUCTORA:** Eida de la Vega nació en La Habana, Cuba, y ahora vive en Nueva Jersey con su madre, su esposo y sus dos hijos. Ha trabajado en Lectorum/Scholastic y, como editora, en la revista *Selecciones del Reader's Digest.*